SPORTS SUPERSTARS

RONALD
ACUÑA JR.

BY THOMAS K. ADAMSON

TORQUE

BELLWETHER MEDIA·MINNEAPOLIS, MN

TORQUE™

Torque brims with excitement perfect for thrill-seekers of all kinds. Discover daring survival skills, explore uncharted worlds, and marvel at mighty engines and extreme sports. In *Torque* books, anything can happen. Are you ready?

This edition first published in 2025 by Bellwether Media, Inc.

No part of this publication may be reproduced in whole or in part without written permission of the publisher. For information regarding permission, write to Bellwether Media, Inc., Attention: Permissions Department, 6012 Blue Circle Drive, Minnetonka, MN 55343.

Library of Congress Cataloging-in-Publication Data

LC record for Ronald Acuña Jr. available at: https://lccn.loc.gov/2024047004

Text copyright © 2025 by Bellwether Media, Inc. TORQUE and associated logos are trademarks and/or registered trademarks of Bellwether Media, Inc.

Editor: Kieran Downs   Designer: Gabriel Hilger

Printed in the United States of America, North Mankato, MN.

TABLE OF CONTENTS

THE 40-70 CLUB	4
WHO IS RONALD ACUÑA JR.?	6
LOVING BASEBALL	8
RISING STAR	12
ACUÑA'S FUTURE	20
GLOSSARY	22
TO LEARN MORE	23
INDEX	24

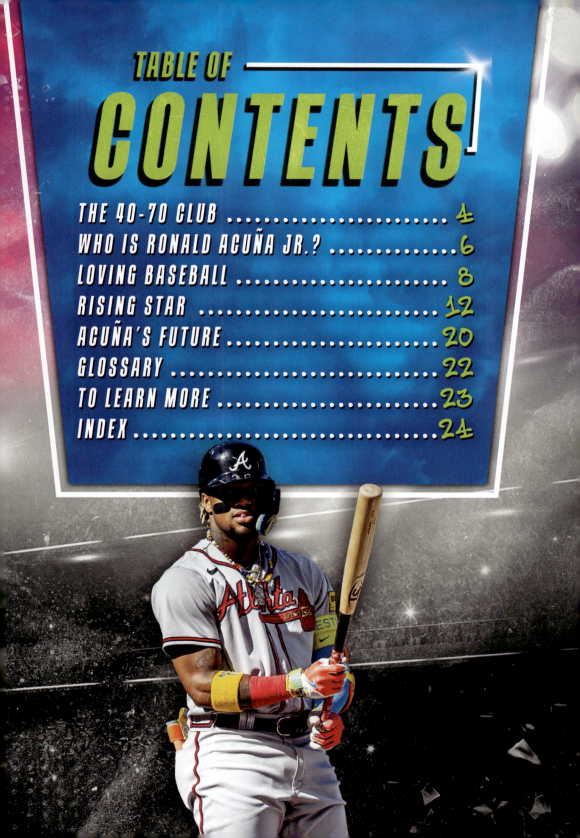

THE 40-70 CLUB

Ronald Acuña Jr. steps off first base. The pitcher winds up. Acuña speeds to second base!

Acuña slides. He touches the base before he gets tagged. It is his 70th **stolen base** of the 2023 season! He is the first player to hit 40 **home runs** and steal 70 bases in one season.

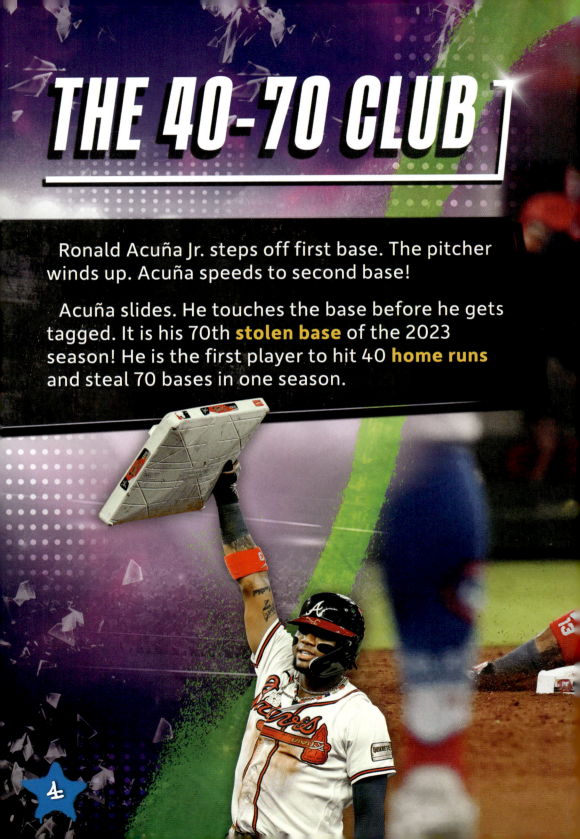

WHO IS RONALD ACUÑA JR.?

Ronald Acuña Jr. is an **outfielder** in **Major League Baseball** (MLB). He plays for the Atlanta Braves. He is a powerful hitter.

La Bestia

Acuña's nickname is *La Bestia*. It means "The Beast" in Spanish.

RONALD ACUÑA JR.

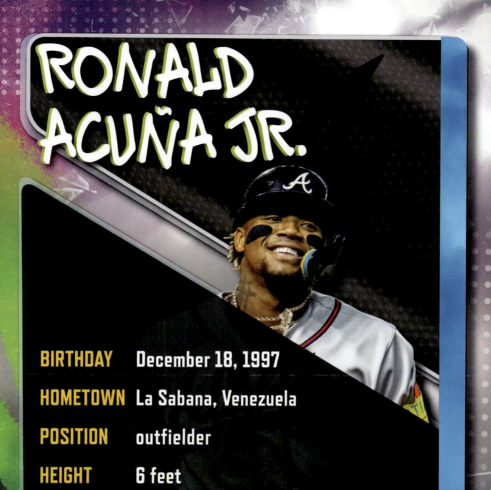

BIRTHDAY	December 18, 1997
HOMETOWN	La Sabana, Venezuela
POSITION	outfielder
HEIGHT	6 feet
SIGNED	Atlanta Braves as an international free agent in 2014

He is also an excellent base runner. He uses his speed to steal bases. Acuña was named the **Most Valuable Player** (MVP) of the **National League** (NL) in 2023.

LOVING BASEBALL

Acuña grew up in Venezuela. Baseball ran in his family. His dad and grandfather played in the **minor leagues**. His uncle and four cousins played in MLB. His brother also plays in MLB.

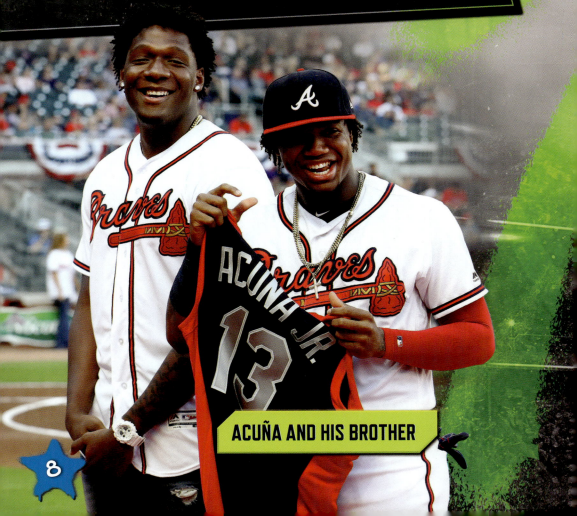

ACUÑA AND HIS BROTHER

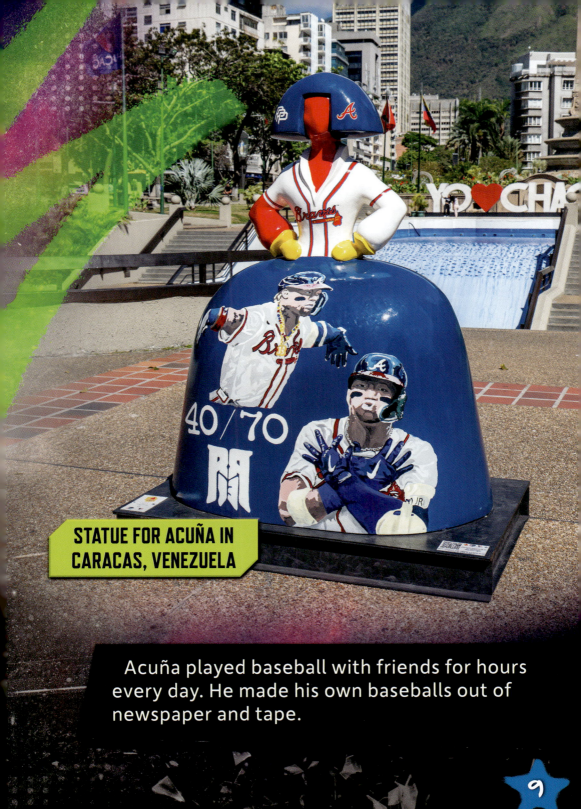

STATUE FOR ACUÑA IN CARACAS, VENEZUELA

Acuña played baseball with friends for hours every day. He made his own baseballs out of newspaper and tape.

As a teenager, Acuña played baseball on a team that traveled across Venezuela. He was getting better and went to many tryouts for **professional** teams. But they never called him back.

When Acuña was 16, a **scout** from the Braves finally noticed his talent. The Braves signed him, and Acuña left for the United States.

FAVORITES

MUSIC GENRE	TEAMMATE	BASEBALL PLAYER	NUMBER
			13
Latin	Ozzie Albies	Miguel Cabrera	13

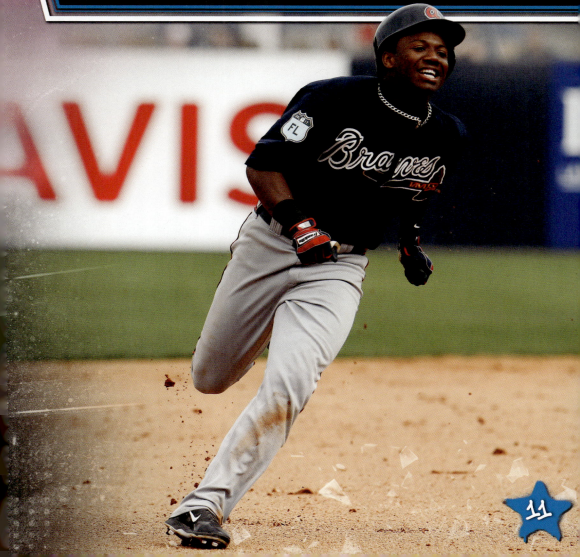

RISING STAR

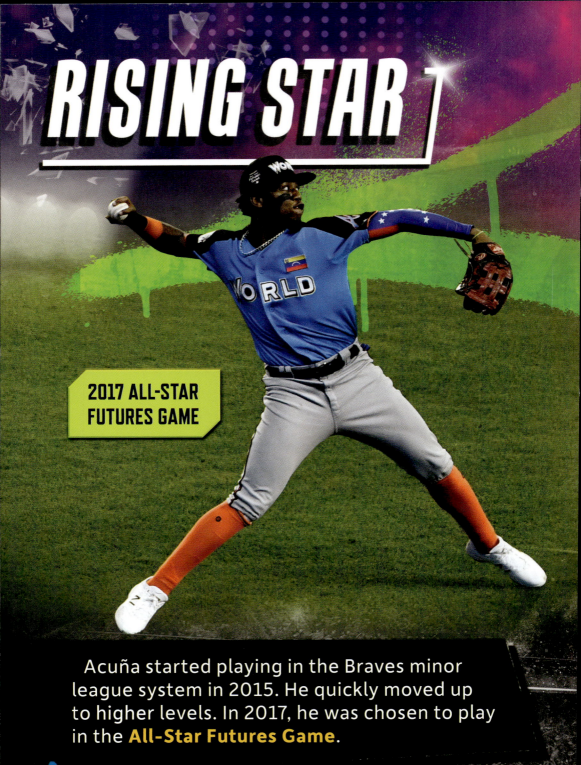

2017 ALL-STAR FUTURES GAME

Acuña started playing in the Braves minor league system in 2015. He quickly moved up to higher levels. In 2017, he was chosen to play in the **All-Star Futures Game**.

12

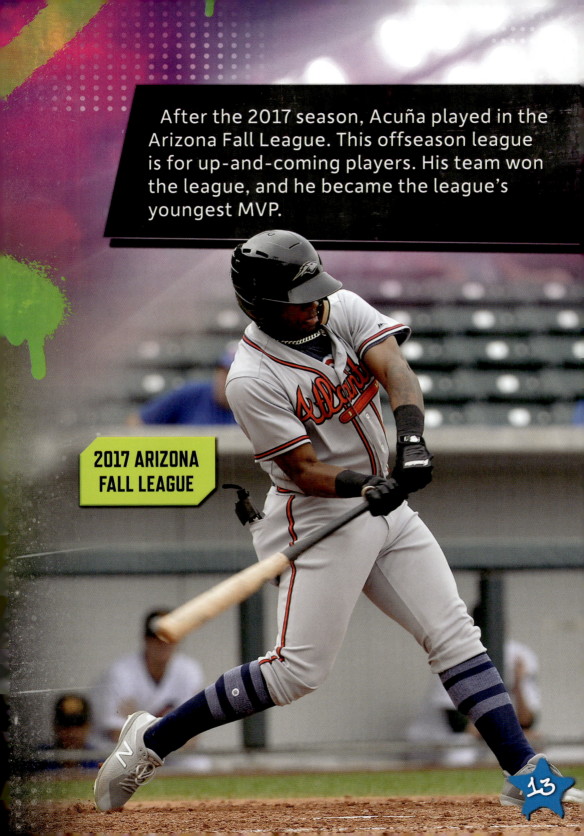

After the 2017 season, Acuña played in the Arizona Fall League. This offseason league is for up-and-coming players. His team won the league, and he became the league's youngest MVP.

2017 ARIZONA FALL LEAGUE

13

2018 NL ROOKIE OF THE YEAR

Acuña was called up to the Braves major league team in 2018. He played well and was named the NL **Rookie** of the Year.

In 2019, Acuña played in his first **All-Star Game**. That season he led the NL in stolen bases with 37. He also hit 41 home runs and won his first **Silver Slugger** award.

Acuña started the 2021 season strong. He hit 24 home runs in just 82 games. But he hurt his knee in July. He was out for the season. The Braves won the **World Series** while he was out.

In 2022, Acuña returned to play. But he did not play as well as he had. His knee was not completely healed.

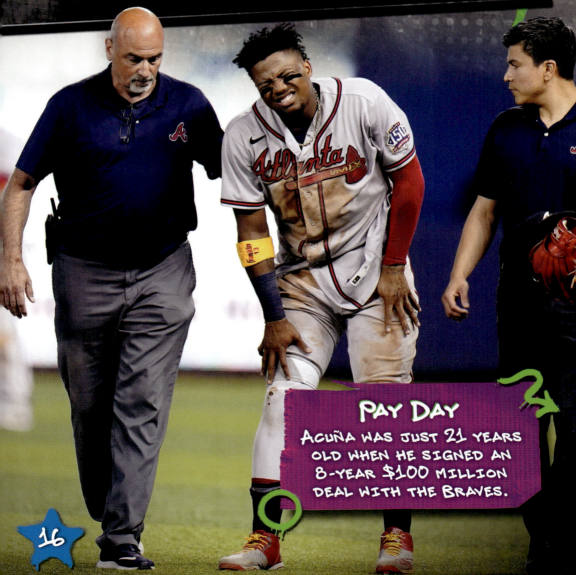

Pay Day

Acuña was just 21 years old when he signed an 8-year $100 million deal with the Braves.

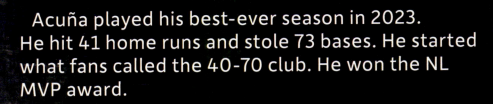

Acuña played his best-ever season in 2023. He hit 41 home runs and stole 73 bases. He started what fans called the 40-70 club. He won the NL MVP award.

Early in the 2024 season, Acuña hurt his other knee. He needed surgery again. He missed the rest of that season.

2023 NL MVP

TIMELINE

April — 2018 —
Acuña plays in his first MLB game

November — 2018 —
Acuña is named the NL Rookie of the Year

— 2019 —
Acuña plays in his first All-Star Game

September 2023

Acuña is the first player to join the 40-70 club

November 2023

Acuña wins the NL MVP Award

ACUÑA'S FUTURE

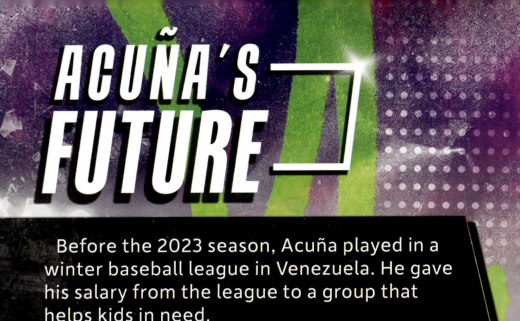

Before the 2023 season, Acuña played in a winter baseball league in Venezuela. He gave his salary from the league to a group that helps kids in need.

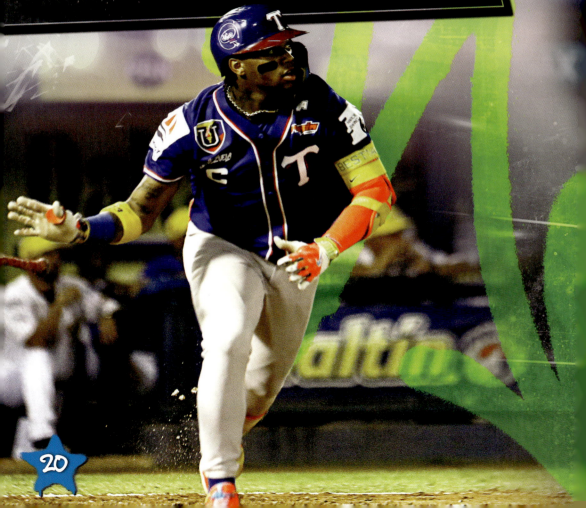

Acuña wants to be in MVP form again. He also wants to help his team win another World Series. The young outfielder still has a bright future!

21

GLOSSARY

All-Star Futures Game—a game featuring the best up-and-coming players in the minor leagues

All-Star Game—a game between the best players in a league

home runs—hits where the batter runs all the way around the bases and scores a run

Major League Baseball— a professional baseball league in the United States; Major League Baseball is often called MLB.

minor leagues—professional baseball leagues below Major League Baseball

Most Valuable Player—the best player in a year, game, or series; the most valuable player is often called the MVP.

National League—one of the two large groupings of teams in Major League Baseball; the other is the American League.

outfielder—a position in baseball in which a player stands far away from the batter to catch hit balls

professional—related to a player or team that makes money playing a sport

rookie—a first-year player in a sports league

scout—a person who watches players in action and recommends them for a team

Silver Slugger—an award recognizing the best hitter of each position in baseball

stolen base—when a baserunner advances safely to the next base without a hit, walk, or error

World Series—the championship series in Major League Baseball, played between the best team in the American League and the best team in the National League

TO LEARN MORE

AT THE LIBRARY

Goodman, Michael E. *Atlanta Braves.* Mankato, Minn.: Creative Education, 2024.

Kaiser, Brianna. *Ronald Acuña Jr. vs. Rickey Henderson: Who Would Win?* Minneapolis, Minn.: Lerner Publications, 2025.

Schwartz, Heather E. *Meet Ronald Acuña Jr.: Atlanta Braves Superstar.* Minneapolis, Minn.: Lerner Publications, 2025.

ON THE WEB

Factsurfer.com gives you a safe, fun way to find more information.

1. Go to www.factsurfer.com

2. Enter "Ronald Acuña Jr." into the search box and click 🔍.

3. Select your book cover to see a list of related content.

INDEX

All-Star Futures Game, 12
All-Star Game, 14, 15
Arizona Fall League, 13
Atlanta Braves, 6, 10, 12, 14, 16, 21
awards, 7, 13, 14, 18
childhood, 8, 9, 10
family, 8
favorites, 11
home runs, 4, 14, 15, 16, 18
hurt, 16, 18
Major League Baseball, 6, 8, 15
map, 15

minor leagues, 8, 12
Most Valuable Player, 7, 13, 18, 21
National League, 7, 14, 18
nickname, 6
outfielder, 6, 21
profile, 7
records, 4, 18
scout, 10
stolen base, 4, 7, 14, 18
timeline, 18–19
trophy shelf, 17
United States, 10
Venezuela, 8, 9, 10, 20
World Series, 16, 21

The images in this book are reproduced through the courtesy of: John Bazemore/ AP Images, cover; Cal Sport Media/ Alamy, pp. 3, 23; Icon Sportswire/ Contributor/ Getty, pp. 4, 11 (Ronald Acuña Jr.), 19; KYDPL KYODO/ AP Images, p. 5; Rich von Biberstein/ Icon Sportswire/ AP Images, p. 6; Kirby Lee/ Alamy, p. 7 (Ronald Acuña Jr.); Tribune Content Agency LLC/ Alamy, pp. 8, 11 (Ozzie Albies); Giongi63, p. 9; Justin K. Aller/ Contributor/ Getty, p. 10; DFree, p. 11 (Latin); Photo Works, p. 11 (Miguel Cabrera); Mark Brown/ Stringer/ Getty Images, p. 12; Jennifer Stewart/ Contributor/ Getty Images, p. 13; Mike Zarrilli/ Contributor/ Getty Images, p. 14; Mr. Lando, p. 15 (Atlanta Braves stadium); Jason Miller/ Stringer/ Getty, p. 15 (2019 MLB All-Star Game); Lynne Sladky/ AP Images, pp. 16, 20; John Bazemore/ AP Images, p. 17; Sarah Stier/ Staff/ Getty Images, p. 18 (2023 NL MVP award); Alex Trautwig/ Stringer/ Getty Images, p. 18 (November 2023); Matt Slocum/ AP Images, p. 21.